A TEEN GUIDE TO SMART CHOICES

by Jane Berthiaume

PublishAmerica
Baltimore

© 2011 by Jane Berthiaume
All rights reserved. No part of this book may be reproduced, stored in a retrieval system or transmitted in any form or by any means without the prior written permission of the publishers, except by a reviewer who may quote brief passages in a review to be printed in a newspaper, magazine or journal.

First printing

This publication contains the opinions and ideas of its author. Author intends to offer information of a general nature. Any reliance on the information herein is at the reader's own discretion.

The author and publisher specifically disclaim all responsibility for any liability, loss, or right, personal or otherwise, which is incurred as a consequence, directly or indirectly, of the use and application of any contents of this book. They further make no representations or warranties with respect to the accuracy or completeness of the contents of this work and specifically disclaim all warranties including without limitation any implied warranty of fitness for a particular purpose. Any recommendations are made without any guarantee on the part of the author or the publisher.

PublishAmerica has allowed this work to remain exactly as the author intended, verbatim, without editorial input.

Hardcover 978-1-4560-4045-1
Softcover 978-1-4560-4046-8
PUBLISHED BY PUBLISHAMERICA, LLLP
www.publishamerica.com
Baltimore

Printed in the United States of America

In loving memory of
John-Michael Mackey,
whose tragic death underscored the importance
of getting this information out to teens.

ACKNOWLEDGEMENTS

This book would not be complete without thanking the people who were instrumental in bringing it about.

First, I'd like to thank my children who have probably been my greatest teachers while they went through the trials and tribulations of their teen years. Also thanks to my husband, Tim, who has always been a great support and encouraged me to follow my dreams.

I'd especially like to thank my test team from Alternative High School who critiqued our workshops and told us straight up what would work and what wouldn't: Sarah, Phil, Christine, Kirsten, Desiree, and a special thanks to John-Michael, who tragically passed away at the age of eighteen.

Thanks to my collaborators, Manon Mitchell and Rosanna Sardella, who helped me develop and deliver the teen workshops to our test team, and Sarah Martensson who worked tirelessly with her camera, capturing the essence of the teens who grace the pages of this book.

Finally, thanks to my Mom, Emily Neilson, from whom I inherited my writing skills. She has always believed in me and my talents, even while I was struggling through academia. She taught me the meaning of unconditional love and support. Thank you!

Table of Contents

PREFACE: **Note to Parents** 9
INTRODUCTION: **Hello, hello, hello…Is There Anybody Out There?** 11
CHAPTER 1: **Why is it so Difficult to be a Teen?** 13
CHAPTER 2: **High on Yourself / Down on Yourself** 19
CHAPTER 3: **Health 101** 26
CHAPTER 4: **Get a Grip on Anxiety** 36
CHAPTER 5: **To Smoke or Not To Smoke** ... 44
CHAPTER 6: **Puff, Puff, Pass** 48
CHAPTER 7: **Relationship Remedy** 54
CHAPTER 8: **Life is Not a Juggling Act** 60
CHAPTER 9: **Listen to Your Intuition** 64
CHAPTER 10: **Wrapping It Up** 74

REFERENCES 76
ABOUT THE AUTHOR 77
ABOUT THE PHOTOGRAPHER/ ILLUSTRATOR 78

PREFACE
Note to Parents

This book is the result of a series of workshops I created for teens. I wanted to put the information developed there into a book for those teens who aren't interested in attending workshops but still want to create positive change in their lives. This book covers topics such as self-esteem, health, anxiety, smoking, drugs, relationships, and listening to one's intuition in order to make good decisions.

I intentionally wanted it to be short enough not to intimidate youthful readers, and small enough to carry around in a backpack. It is to be used as a teen's "go to" book, and I anticipate it will be referred to often.

It is important that this teen guide be shared and read by both you and your teen. I encourage you to read through these pages and interact and communicate with your teen. My hope is that it will spark discussions on some very difficult subjects and situations. When your teen is better prepared for challenging situations, both of you will have the confidence to trust each other more.

You will also find in this book many exercises and facts that I hope will be of interest and benefit to you. My discussion of brain development in Chapter 1, for example, may give you a new perspective on the demands and expectations we sometimes place on our teens. You may also benefit from the various exercises to battle anxiety and stress, which most adults have in their lives.

Please take the time to discuss the topics in this book with your teen. It will dramatically enhance the quality of life of each member of your family. Build an open and close relationship with your teen today, so he or she will feel comfortable enough to turn to you tomorrow.

This little book can help you do that.

INTRODUCTION

Hello, hello, hello...
Is There Anybody Out There?

This was the question my two teenage sons asked when they were facing typical teenage problems and had seemingly nowhere to turn for help or advice. My situation growing up was much different from theirs. I grew up in a two-parent home with seven siblings, whereas my kids grew up with just each other and a single mom. So this was all new territory for them and for me. Needless to say, we encountered quite a few challenges.

We looked everywhere we could for help, but unless a teen is ready to harm him—or herself, or is addicted to some sort of substance, there is little help to be found. This was most discouraging as these are the years when teens make decisions that will alter the course of their lives.

In our case, we were forced to just bumble through and make our mistakes along the way, but I want to offer a better way for you and your parents. That is why I wrote this book. There *are* people and resources out there that can steer you in the right direction, so...

Get ready to say goodbye to the person you once were. This little book has a big message and will open your eyes to a world of possibilities.

Ideally, I would like you and your parents to read this book together as a family. It is meant to be shared, discussed, passed around, debated, and used to change your life *and* your way of thinking. If everyone is on the "same page", so to speak, the information in this book will be even more effective.

My hope is for this to be the rattiest, dirtiest, most marked up and highlighted book on your shelf. I want this to be your "go to" book. Refer to it often and read it again and again. Everyone can use a refresher now and then, so turn to whatever chapter is relevant when issues crop up. You can even share it with a friend when they come to you for advice.

Not only have I condensed my thoughts and knowledge of forty-five years into this little book, but I have also consulted many very knowledgeable teens during the writing of it. *A Teen Guide to Smart Choices* is short and to the point. My intention is to get you thinking outside the box and introduce you to a way of life that is more in line with where you want to go and what you want to do. I want you to be prepared to make the best possible decisions for your future and your life. I want you to think about what you stand for and what you won't stand for.

I'd like you now to stuff this book into your bookbag or backpack and read it whenever you're riding the transit or travelling anywhere. Read it when you're alone eating lunch, in bed at night, or just relaxing in the park. Besides, I heard that people tend to think you're more intriguing when they see you reading a book.

CHAPTER 1

Why is it so Difficult to be a Teen?

Actually, there are physiological reasons the teen years are so difficult. It has to do with the brain and how it develops. For instance, did you know your brain doesn't fully mature until your early to mid-20s?

BRAIN DEVELOPMENT

Brain maturation begins at the back, in the cerebellum. This area of the brain controls physical coordination which aids in the development of skills like balance and manual dexterity. The front of the brain, called the prefrontal cortex, is the last area of the brain to fully mature. This area, sometimes called the area of "sober second thought", is responsible for planning, clear thinking, impulse control, and higher-level reasoning. The fact that these higher-level functions of the prefrontal cortex have not fully developed in teens accounts—especially under stressful and emotional circumstances—for much impulsive behaviour and poor decision making. (Giedd, 2009; Winters, 2008)

Does this mean that there is something wrong with your brain? That you are somehow unable to think clearly and reason? Not at all. As a matter of fact, it means your brain is growing and changing, creating new neural connections, and more refined, efficient, and sophisticated circuitry to help you deal with future challenges. However, it is a process, and you must learn to deal with sometimes impulsive, risky behaviour and volatile emotions. You need to stop and think about the consequences of your actions, and make sure you neither harm yourself nor anyone else.

The teen years will make a lot more sense and run much more smoothly when both you and your parents are aware of and understand these basic facts of biology. They will also allow you to be a little more tolerant of each other. For example, parents must understand that good judgment, self-control, and the ability to consider and foresee consequences are skills that are growing and developing in their teen.

THE TEEN PERSPECTIVE

Here is what some teens have to say about why these years can be so difficult. My first volunteer is an 18-year-old male—

I'll call him Wesley—who currently goes to an alternative high school.

I asked him: "In your opinion, what is the toughest part about being a teen?"

Wesley took no time in answering. "Nobody listens," he said.

He felt too that the school system was letting him down. After having failed at a traditional Catholic school, he decided to go to an alternative high school. The teacher/student ratio at the alternative school was lower, the atmosphere was more relaxed—the teachers even allowed students to listen to music while they worked—and, as Wesley put it, "The teachers are more chill."

However, even the alternative system has its drawbacks. The school is very small, just over 100 students, and the range of courses offered is extremely limited. Wesley's frustration continues to build as he repeatedly asks anyone who will listen: "Why can't anyone teach a course that is relevant to what I want to do with my life? Teach me how to apply for a mortgage, or how to shop for groceries and get the best deals. What about explaining how I go about renting an apartment or creating a budget? Teach me how to plant a garden, cut the grass, or do a load of laundry. I need life skills; I don't need to know the cosine or the tangent of an angle."

The aggravation that Wesley feels with the school system has caused his stomach to become irritated, and he can no longer get up in the morning without having a couple of hours of stomach pain. He no longer wants to go to school and is in jeopardy of dropping out and not getting his high school diploma.

Wesley truly wants to learn, but he just doesn't want to waste his time on what he considers to be useless material. If it's something he can use in life, he is all for learning and putting the time and effort into the course. He already has a career path in mind; he wants to be a sound engineer, but there are no courses available in this field at the alternative school.

So what do we do with a system that's inflexible and a student who's frustrated?

Since it's easier to help one individual than try to change a whole institution, I opted to address Wesley's stomach issues first. I started with some natural healing to deal with the emotions Wesley was suppressing. If you don't allow your emotions to come to the surface, they will simply fester and come out in other ways. For Wesley, his bottled up emotions surfaced as stomach pain.

Wesley is now doing more research into other learning alternatives so he can take courses more relevant to his needs, even if that means going back to a more traditional high school, or paying for online courses.

My second volunteer is a 16-year-old, highly intelligent, highly successful young woman. Some might consider her an overachiever. We'll call her Beth.

Beth also took very little time answering my question; however, her answer was quite different from Wesley's. Beth's difficulties lie in dealing with peer and parental pressure. Her life is full of challenging subjects at school, extracurricular sports, family obligations, and, of course, a boyfriend. Sometimes she finds all of this difficult to handle and even overwhelming.

Her parents expect good grades from her in every subject, including the ones that don't really interest her and are not her forte. Nothing less than being on the honour roll is acceptable to them. She also has the added challenge of being an excellent athlete; she is expected to perform on the soccer field while still holding an exceptional grade point average. This can be a lot of pressure for someone who is also a pleaser. She doesn't want to let anyone down, including herself, and has set her own goals and expectations for her life.

Parents' expectations are not the only problem. She feels an extreme amount of pressure from friends who want her to experience new things, like drugs and alcohol, and engage in sometimes risky behaviours. There is a lot of pressure to "fit in". Beth feels that her friends sometimes look down on her, and this can cause her to make what she considers to be stupid decisions that she later regrets.

My suggestion to Beth on how to deal with peer and parental pressure is to first determine what she stands for. There is an old saying: "You've got to stand for something or you'll stand for anything." Make a list of your deal breakers and live by them. For example, if smoking pot is not something that you see as a way to get you to your goals, then don't do it and stick to your guns. If you need a little less extracurricular activity, then communicate this to your parents. Not everyone is going to be, or wants to be, an Olympic level athlete; perhaps you just want to join a recreational league. Life is all about having fun while trying not to hurt anyone else in the process. Try not to be afraid to communicate your needs to either your parents or your friends. I have discovered that when you are honest with people and speak from the heart, they genuinely appreciate it and don't tend to hold it against you. Try speaking your truth from the heart; you may be surprised at the reaction you get.

CHAPTER 2

High on Yourself / Down on Yourself

What's it going to be? Do you want to live a life loving yourself or hating yourself?

Have counsellors, parents, teachers, or friends ever told you that you need to raise your self-esteem, or not to be so hard on yourself? If so, this is the chapter you need to pay extra special attention to. I will tell you how to raise your self-esteem, love yourself more, and increase your tolerance of others.

ACCEPTING ALL ASPECTS OF YOUR PERSONALITY

Self-esteem means accepting both the *light* and the *dark* sides of your personality. The dark side, sometimes called the shadow side, is that aspect of your personality that you reject as bad. The light side, in contrast, is that aspect of your personality that you like or consider good. Beliefs about there being good and bad parts to our personalities have been around a long, long time. In fact, many of these beliefs we have simply accepted from others. They were passed on to us by our parents, friends, clergy, TV, radio, and many other outside forces. The truth is that what we perceive to be good and bad parts of our personalities are actually all good, and vitally important to who we really are.

Let's consider the supposed "dark" side of your personality. You can usually recognize its characteristics by identifying what bothers you or what triggers you in others. This concept is called *mirroring*. When you see something in someone else that annoys you, it's actually an aspect of your own personality that you consider ugly or weak.

Imagine an individual bothered by someone who exhibits traits of passivity or shyness. These traits are typically viewed as signs of weakness. If someone is acting scared or weak, and this irritates you, then passivity is an aspect of your personality that you think is bad. It is a part of your "dark" side that you try to hide from the rest of the world. The problem with not accepting this part of your personality is that sometimes you need to call on this shy or passive part of yourself. Let's say, for example, someone starts getting up in your face and wants to start a fight. In this case, you may want to call on that nonaggressive side of your personality to talk yourself out of the situation and avoid the fight.

RAISING YOUR SELF-ESTEEM

So, let me tell you in one simple sentence how to raise your self-esteem. Listen very carefully: You raise your self-esteem by recognizing, embracing, and ultimately loving all aspects of yourself. People tend to repress the "dark" side of their personalities because they think it's bad; however, it's possible to acknowledge and accept your so-called weaknesses and turn them into hidden strengths.

In order to raise your self-esteem (using the example of passivity), you must

1. **Recognize the trigger**—Notice your reaction; see that you are annoyed by another person's passivity.
2. **Turn it around**—Remember how this same passive behaviour has helped you in your own life, perhaps to avoid fights or doing something stupid, by "chickening out".
3. **Embrace your passivity**—Laugh about it, be proud of it, and accept it. When you accept it in yourself, you will also accept it in others. This will make you much more tolerant of others.

Repressing what you consider your undesirable personality traits will only cause them to become bottled up and emerge at inappropriate moments. They are all good and can help you to become more yourself, a more complete person. Perhaps you *need* to get a little angry when you feel you're being taken advantage of, perhaps it's *okay* to brag a little during a job interview, or perhaps it's safe and even *appropriate* to be a little emotional at a funeral. These are proper expressions of your so-called *dark* traits. Remember too that these emotions are what make us both human *and* interesting.

CIRCLE OF CONTROL

Understanding clearly what it is you can and cannot control in your life will help you improve your self-esteem. It's senseless to beat yourself up for something that isn't even in your realm of control.

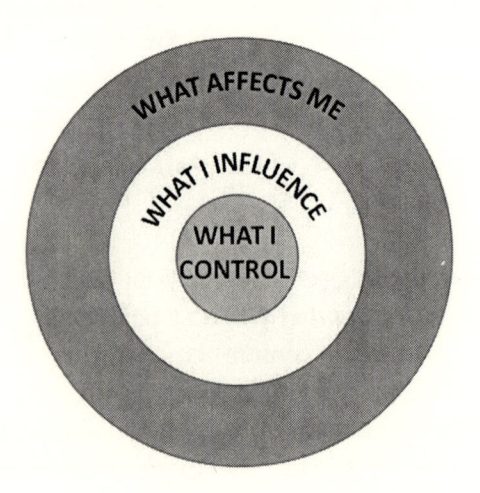

(Diagram: concentric circles labeled WHAT AFFECTS ME, WHAT I INFLUENCE, WHAT I CONTROL)

The simple drawing below will help you understand this concept and explain what is in your circle of control.

What Affects Me: Gravity, the weather, the price of goods, other people's choices and behaviour

What I Influence: Everything and everyone I come into contact with—to varying degrees

What I Control: My thoughts, my feelings, and my actions

There are many things in your life over which you have no control, for example, the weather. You may be affected by the weather—a dark and rainy day may depress you, or a bright and sunny day may make you happy—but you only have control over your reaction to it. Perhaps you look outside and see the rain pouring down, forming mud puddles on the sidewalk. You say to yourself: "Oh man, where did I leave my umbrella? I'm going to look like a total jerk running for the bus stop, trying not to get wet and ruining my good hair day."

We can, however, choose to turn those thoughts around and say: "Sweet! Where did I put my rubber boots and rain gear? I love the rain. I should have been born a duck." Nothing has changed about the situation except your thoughts and your attitude. How do you want to live your life—being miserable or being happy? Remember, all you can control are *your* thoughts, *your* feelings, and *your* actions.

There are, however, many things in your life that you can and do influence. You can, of course, influence people and situations by expressing your opinion, by being a good role model, and by standing up for what you believe in. Friends influence each other. Because we enjoy being with them, we are more open to their ideas. Friends often influence what music we listen to, what movies we watch, and what social networking sites we join. However, you still don't have any real control over what others do. Remember, they may not take your advice or follow your ideas, and that's okay; you have no control over that. Be content with letting them know how you feel, and then let it go at that. My advice is not to worry about how people react to your influence.

When you try to influence someone else, or try to control a situation, pay special attention to the difference between influence and control. Think of the circles and what you can influence and control, and think, feel, and act accordingly. If you are thinking: "I wish this person would do this", or "How can I make so-and-so do that", then stop what you are doing! You do not have the control to make another person do anything. Remember too that neither can anyone control you. Your decisions are yours, and yours alone. So listen to the advice of people around you, and make the best decisions you can for yourself.

HANDLING CRITICISM

Handling criticism, or self-criticism, can be extremely difficult for someone with low self-esteem. By self-criticism I mean that voice inside your head that keeps sending you negative messages like "You can't do that", or "That was a stupid thing to do". Don't panic; we all have that little voice, and it can be very annoying and counterproductive if we listen to it.

Here's what to do when faced with criticism, whether from yourself or someone else. The first step is to question it. Ask yourself, "Is this true?" The next step is to act on this information. If the criticism is true, you may want to change your behaviour. If the criticism is not true, simply ignore it, because it shouldn't affect you. Move on, and let it go; it is merely someone else's opinion.

Say someone tells you that you are drinking too much. You must ask yourself honestly, "Is this true?" Think about it without becoming defensive. Does your drinking cause problems at school, at work, at home, with your relationships, or with your health? If it's causing significant consequences in any of these areas, and you are still choosing to drink, then seek help and start making some changes. However, if you only have the odd social drink and rarely get drunk, then this is someone overreacting and you should choose to ignore the criticism. If it isn't part of your reality and your truth, then it doesn't affect you; it's their issue.

I am going to squeeze in one more very important tip for keeping your self-esteem high, and that is to ask for help whenever you need it. If you find yourself getting frustrated, there is no shame in asking for help. It's foolish to sit and bang your head against the wall when there are lots of people happy to give you advice or their opinion on something. Turn to someone you trust, or call a helpline. Do whatever you need to do to keep yourself healthy and happy.

CHAPTER 3

Health 101

A healthy lifestyle is every bit as important to a teen as it is to an adult. To be effective, it must be approached on four fronts simultaneously.

1. Nutrition—The fresher (non-packaged, non-processed) foods you can put into your body, the better your health will be. Only you can control what you put in your mouth!

2. Exercise—Get out there and move; do something fun: dance, walk, ski, whatever you enjoy, but get outside and get your body moving. Exercise helps with anxiety, depression, and your overall health.

3. **Sleep**—This is one of the most overlooked aspects of health, especially by teens. Teens need a lot of quality sleep as their bodies go through this period of extreme hormonal change. It is when you are asleep that your body heals.

4. **Mental Health**—This really comes down to making yourself happy. It's important to do something just for yourself every day. Take a bath, read a book, listen to music, meditate, play a musical instrument, or sit by a crackling fire. Do whatever brings you joy. You are responsible for your own happiness.

TAKING RESPONSIBILITY FOR YOUR OWN HEALTH

As a teen approaching adulthood, it is your responsibility to take care of your own health. It is important to see your doctor annually, and not just when you are sick or having a health issue. (See the end of this chapter for tips on nutrition, exercise, and sleep.)

There are also alternative forms of health care available, known as energy healing, which are based on Eastern medicine. These natural healing techniques are particularly useful as they focus more on preventive health care—preventing illness in the first place, rather than having to cure it. As a Registered Clinical Hypnotherapist, I am partial to these techniques. I have trained in many healing modalities, including Healing Touch and PSYCH-K.

ALTERNATIVE HEALTH CARE

Energy healing can take many forms. Have you heard of Reiki, Guided Meditation, Healing Touch, Body Talk, or perhaps Yoga? These, and many other modalities, are different types of energy healing. Let me explain what energy healing is.

The human body has seven main points running down its centre called "chakra" points. When these seven areas of the body are open, they keep the energy flowing through your system. When the energy flows properly, it boosts the immune system and keeps you healthy. When these points are closed off or the flow of energy is restricted, the blockage acts much like a kink in a hose. This can cause a slowing down of the energy flow, compromising the immune system and inviting disease.

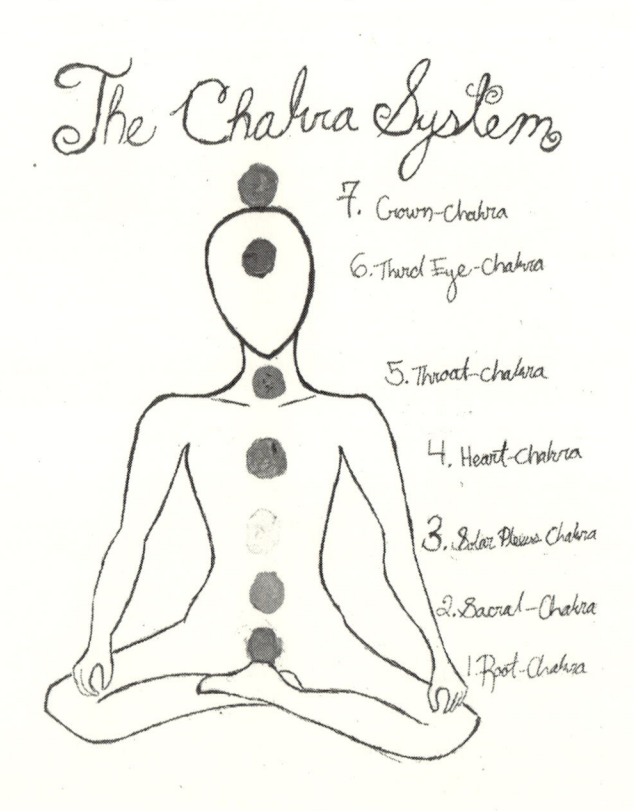

The Chakra System

7. Crown-Chakra
6. Third Eye-Chakra
5. Throat-Chakra
4. Heart-Chakra
3. Solar Plexus Chakra
2. Sacral-Chakra
1. Root-Chakra

The object of energy healing, in all its healing modalities, is to keep these seven main chakras open. The chakra points are called the crown, third eye, throat, heart, solar plexus, sacral, and root. There is nothing mystical or magical about energy healing. The practitioner simply opens up the chakra points to allow the energy to flow so the body can attain its optimal state to heal itself. You simply need to find a modality that works for you, as everyone responds differently to the various energy healing treatments.

Fifteen years ago I was diagnosed with psoriasis. The doctors told me there were treatments available, but no cure for the disease. For many years I followed their treatment plan with no success. Luckily, I wasn't buying what the doctors were selling, and I started searching for other ways to rid myself of this distressing disease. After years of research and trying many different modalities, I finally succeeded through a combination of Healing Touch and PSYCH-K. Healing Touch helped heal my body, and PSYCH-K healed my mind and made me believe I could actually be rid of this disease. I am happy to report that after four years, I am still psoriasis-free! Seeing is believing. My successful treatment led me to begin my studies of natural and alternative healing.

My advice is never to let an unacceptable diagnosis keep you from reaching your highest healing potential. Seek out an energy healer to help you with physical, emotional, and spiritual healing.

NUTRITIONAL TIPS CHECKLIST

- Eat a healthy breakfast within two hours of waking to get your metabolism going. Studies have shown that people who don't eat breakfast consume more calories throughout the day.

- Eat 3 well-balanced meals per day, consisting of half a plate of vegetables, a quarter plate of meat or protein, and a quarter plate of whole grains or starch (brown rice, whole grain pasta, whole grain bread, etc.). A standard plate is about the size of a Frisbee.

- Make sure the protein portion of your meal is the size of your palm—lean meats and fish are best. The proper portion size of whole grain or starch is one-half cup of cooked brown rice, 1 ounce of whole grain bread, or a mini bagel. Whole grain foods are high in fibre and reduce the number of calories absorbed during digestion. You need 4 to 5 servings of fruits and vegetables per day. A proper portion size of vegetables is 1 cup of leafy greens such as lettuce or spinach, or one-half cup of celery, cauliflower, broccoli, mushrooms, tomato, or similar vegetables.

- Eat 2 to 3 snacks per day to sustain you between meals so you don't overeat at mealtime. If you eat at regular intervals, your body will tend not to store fat. A healthy snack could be a handful of grapes, a handful of nuts/seeds, or a snack-sized yogurt. Good nutrition takes planning, so make sure you have healthy snacks on hand that are easy to take with you.

• Take your time when eating. Put your fork down between bites and talk to your family. It takes 20 minutes for your brain to catch up with your stomach and realize you are full. Pay attention, and enjoy what you're eating, and turn the TV off!

• Replace soda pop and juice with water. You'd be amazed how much sugar and how many calories are in these drinks. If water bores you, then jazz it up with a squeeze of lemon or a wedge of orange. I have a peppermint plant from which I pick a few leafs that I put in my water; it's all natural, and peppermint aids the digestion too.

• Limit your intake of desserts and junk food. I know these foods are tempting, and it's okay to indulge once in a while, but try having a bite or a sliver of pie, rather than an entire piece. If you have to have some chips or something else a little naughty, keep it to a handful, and keep the rest of the bag out of reach and out of sight.

• Choose healthy alternatives when eating out. Most fast-food places now have healthy choices on their menu, so be smart and place a healthy order. Be conscious of portion sizes, as they can be quite large. I typically cut my wrap/sandwich/burger in half and bring the rest home. This way I can treat myself twice, or share with my family.

• Stay around the perimeter of the grocery store when shopping. You'll notice this is where all the fresh produce, meats, and dairy products are. The inside aisles are loaded with packaged and preserved foods which should generally be avoided. Also take a list with you of the items you will need for the week, and limit yourself to those!

• Look for the freshest and brightest coloured fruits and vegetables when shopping. These contain the most vitamins and minerals. If it looks bad, it *is* bad. Don't waste your money. Look for items like blueberries, dark green veggies, cherries, etc. The fresher and more beautiful they are, the more appetizing they will be.

EXERCISE TIPS CHECKLIST

• Exercise doesn't have to be something you dread or something you feel you have to do. Why not make it fun? Participate in an activity you enjoy and think a little outside the box. Try your hand at yoga, archery, hiking, kayaking, breakdancing, whatever gets you off the couch and your heart rate up.

• Exercise is great as a natural stress reliever. Stress is the leading cause of a whole list of diseases, so get active, feel good, and prevent illness, all at the same time.

• Getting exercise can be as simple as taking the stairs instead of the elevator, walking instead of driving, or picking the furthest parking spot from your destination. You'll be surprised at how many extra calories you can burn, just by adding a little activity to your daily routine.

• It's important to fuel your body before starting a workout. Eat a light snack of fruit, yogurt, veggies, or a handful of nuts and seeds about an hour or so before exercising.

- The human body is between 55 and 78 percent water, depending on your age. Our bodies require water for cell regeneration, digestion, flushing out toxins, cushioning joints, preventing dehydration and maintaining proper metabolism. You'll need to drink before, during, and after exercising. Approximately 2 litres of water is the daily requirement.

- It's important to incorporate strength training, cardio, and stretching into your workouts. Strength training helps raise your metabolism and strengthens your bones. Cardio helps you burn fat and decreases your risk for heart disease. Stretching helps improve range of motion and prevent injuries. A combination of all three is best for overall health and wellness.

- Make sure to challenge yourself so you don't get bored. Mix up the routine a little and throw in some interesting challenges. In sports you always want to play a better team to help you improve. The same principle applies to exercise. Push yourself a little more each time. Add a few reps each week to your workout, or try a light jog for a few blocks the next time you're out for a walk.

- Be sure to set goals for yourself. Short-term goals will keep you moving forward. Challenge yourself with a new activity once you've gotten to a desired fitness level. Maybe you'll start with the goal of doing a 2-kilometer hike, then move on to a kickboxing class, and who knows, maybe eventually a triathlon. You choose how far you want to take your fitness, but try to keep to a daily routine.

- Don't overdo it, though, especially when first starting an exercise regime. If your muscles are extremely sore the next day, you'll be less likely to want to exercise again.

- Schedule your workouts. This makes it harder to make excuses. There are lots of exercise options in this checklist, so get busy and get active.

SLEEP TIPS CHECKLIST

- A regular sleep schedule is key to a successful night's sleep. The body needs to keep a consistent wake time and bedtime, even on the weekends. Avoid napping and sleeping in, as this throws off your sleep/wake cycle. If you must nap, keep it to 20 or 30 minutes and only when absolutely necessary.

- Create a space that is conducive to sleeping. Be sure your bed is comfortable and free of clutter. Keep your room cool, pull the shades down to make it dark, and close the door to avoid noise and interruptions. You may even play a little soothing music.

- Create a bedtime ritual designed to put you in the mood for sleep. Read a book, take a bath or shower, meditate, do a progressive relaxation or breathing exercise, or even write in your journal. Try to do the same ritual each night to signal the body that it's time to relax and prepare for sleep.

- Remove the TV, computer, or game console from your bedroom. You should only associate your bedroom with sleeping. Keep the electronics out and the peace and serenity in!

If you can't remove these items from your bedroom, at least refrain from using them an hour or so before bedtime.

- If you can't get to sleep after all this preparation, then leave the bedroom. You should be able to fall asleep within 15 minutes. If you can't, try another relaxing activity outside the bedroom for a few minutes and then try again. I sometimes find it helpful to jot down the thoughts that are keeping me awake and perhaps create a to-do list to get the thoughts off my mind.

- To give you the best opportunity to sleep through the night, avoid eating or drinking too close to bedtime. Overeating will make your stomach uncomfortable and drinking can cause you to wake in the night for a trip to the washroom.

- This is one time I'm not going to tell you to exercise. Exercising within 3 hours of bedtime can stimulate you and make it difficult to fall asleep. Try exercising in the morning instead. Overheating your body with exercise or too hot a bath or shower can make sleeping difficult.

- There are a few stimulants you should avoid at least 6 hours before going to bed. The first of these is caffeine, contained in coffee, tea, soft drinks, and chocolate. The next stimulant is nicotine. Some smokers experience withdrawal symptoms during the night, which can disturb normal sleep. Nicotine can also make it difficult to fall asleep and wake up, not to mention give you nightmares. It's best to avoid smoking altogether, in my opinion. The last stimulant I want to mention is alcohol. Although many people think of alcohol as a sedative, it actually has the opposite effect and disrupts your sleep.

CHAPTER 4

Get a Grip on Anxiety

When you're feeling anxious, it's a signal from your body that you're living in fear.

In this chapter I will teach you ways to get a grip on your anxiety. You will learn various exercises to quiet the fight-or-flight response and get you out of living in fear. They will include, among others, a breathing technique, progressive relaxation, and meditation to help reduce fear-based mind chatter.

RELAXATION BREATHING 4-7-8

The first exercise is called *relaxation breathing 4-7-8*. It is very simple, takes almost no time, requires no equipment, and can be done virtually anywhere. Although you can do this exercise in any position, I'd like you, while you are learning to do it, to be seated in a chair with your back straight. Place the tip of your tongue against the ridge of tissue just behind your upper front teeth, and keep it there throughout the exercise. You will be exhaling through your mouth around your tongue; try pursing your lips slightly if this seems awkward.

- Exhale completely through your mouth, making a whoosh sound.
- Close your mouth and inhale quietly through your nose for a mental count of **four**.
- Hold your breath for a count of **seven**.
- Exhale completely through your mouth, making a whoosh sound for a count of **eight**.
- This is one breath. Now inhale again and repeat the cycle three more times for a total of four breaths.

Note: you should inhale quietly through your nose and exhale audibly through your mouth. The tip of your tongue stays in position the whole time. Exhaling should take twice as long as inhaling. The time you spend on each phase is not important; the ratio of 4:7:8, however, is important. If you have trouble holding your breath, speed up the exercise by counting faster but keep to the ratio of 4:7:8 for the three phases. With practice, you can slow it all down and get used to inhaling and exhaling more and more deeply.

This exercise is a natural tranquilizer for the nervous system. Unlike tranquilizing drugs, which are often effective when you first take them, but then lose their power over time, this exercise is subtle when you first try it, but gains in power with repetition and practice. Try practicing this exercise at least twice a day in the beginning. You cannot do it too frequently. Do not do more than four breaths at one time for the first month of practice. Later, if you wish, you can extend it to eight breaths. If you feel a little lightheaded when you first breathe this way, do not be concerned; it will pass.

Once you develop this technique by practicing it every day, it will become a very useful tool that you will always have with you. Use it whenever anything upsetting happens—before you react. Use it whenever you are aware of internal tension, like perhaps when you are preparing to write an exam or compete in a competitive sport. Use it to help you fall asleep. Go ahead and teach this exercise to others; everyone can benefit from it, and it's easy.

This is just one of many types of breathing exercises, so if this doesn't float your boat, than do some research on the Internet and find a technique that works for you. The most important thing is that you learn to breathe more deeply to slow down your heart rate. A slower heart rate is a signal to the rest of your body that the danger has passed and you can relax again. Find the technique that works for you.

PROGRESSIVE RELAXATION

Another great exercise is called *progressive relaxation*. Put simply, it is a technique to relax the muscles, starting at the head or scalp and moving down the entire body right to the bottom of the feet. I like to use this one in bed at night, especially if I'm having trouble getting to sleep. Some people do this exercise starting at the feet and moving to the top of the head, so do whichever feels more natural to you.

If you have trouble relaxing your muscles, start by tensing up the muscle for a few seconds, and then relaxing it. Here is the order you can follow:
- Scalp
- Face
- Jaw
- Neck
- Shoulders
- Chest
- Abdomen
- Spine
- Arms
- Hands
- Thighs
- Calves
- Feet

Remember to keep your breathing relaxed as you relax your muscles. Relaxing your muscles takes a little practice at first, but when you get good at it, you can just think the word *relax,* and the muscles automatically relax.

MEDITATION

Meditation is a very effective way to deal with anxiety and may even improve your health and spiritual development.

The object of meditation is to put your focus on one area. When people first begin to meditate, this seems to be their biggest challenge. They find it difficult to quiet the mind chatter. Buddhists call your inner voice "a crazy monkey". This "crazy monkey" whispering in your ear all day can make it tough to focus.

With this in mind, it's important to first set an intention or a focus for your meditation. The clearer and more specific you are with your intention, the better the results of the meditation will be. For example, don't set an intention to speak with your guides or angels that is too vague. Set the intention for your angels or guides to provide guidance on something specific, such as a problem you're currently facing, or a career path decision you need to make.

Also, choose a place to meditate that is quiet, away from distractions, and where you won't be disturbed. You can't concentrate if you're worried about your cellphone ringing, or the cat jumping into your lap, or someone coming to the door. Commit to taking this time for yourself and not letting any distractions take away your focus.

If you wish to explore the subject in more detail, there are plenty of meditation CDs and meditation groups that you can use to guide you through the process. If you wish to start right now, follow these simple guidelines I have developed.

    1. Prepare your space—Select a quiet place where you will not be interrupted.
    2. Light a candle—This attracts your guides and angels into the space.

3. **Close your eyes**—If you don't like to close your eyes, pick a point of focus in the room, like the lit candle.
4. **Relaxation breathing**—Start by taking some deep breaths to slow down your heart rate.
5. **Progressive relaxation**—Relax the muscles in your body from head to toe.
6. **Create a safe place**—Visualize or feel yourself in a place where you are completely comfortable and safe. It can be indoors or outdoors, as long as it's a place where you can relax.
7. **Invite in your angels or guides**—I find it helpful to have spirits or mentors with me to guide me through the meditation and to help when I am seeking knowledge.
8. **Allow the journey to begin**—Try not to expect too much; just be open to whatever comes. Don't judge and cut off the flow of information; just allow whatever comes.
9. **Be thankful**—Thank your angels and guides for coming, and be thankful for the exchange of information. If you didn't get very much, be patient and practice often. It will get easier.

You may want to play some relaxation music while you meditate, but be careful not to pick music with words, as this can be distracting. Pick music that has nature sounds, or drumming. Music can really set the mood for the meditation.

Bear in mind that this is my particular way of meditating. There is no right or wrong way to meditate; you do what works and what is relaxing for you. Again, these are merely guidelines. Relax and enjoy the experience.

FEAR-BASED MIND CHATTER

In dealing with fear-based mind chatter, you need to ask yourself the same question you ask when someone is criticizing you: Is it true? Whatever story you're making up in your head is probably twenty times worse than what is actually happening. For example, you may be thinking, "Oh my God, that guy's totally looking at me. I think he's checking me out. Do I have a booger or something? What would he want with me? I'm not even in his league." Meanwhile, the guy totally thinks you're hot.

Okay, that story was supposed to be humorous, but we do tend to create stories in our minds that aren't real. Be careful of these stories because they can have you living in fear, especially if your mind chatter is like the next example that a parent may experience. "Where the heck is Johnny? He was supposed to be home a half an hour ago. I can't get through on his cellphone; he probably got drunk, crashed the car, and is lying in a ditch somewhere." Just then Johnny comes walking through the door. "Oh sorry, Mom, my cellphone died so I couldn't reach you to tell you I was running a little late."

When you start creating those negative stories in your head, stop them right away and change your thinking: "Johnny's probably fine; he's a pretty responsible kid but sometimes loses track of time, so I'll give him another hour before I start to track him down or get worked up." You can simply change the thoughts in your head to something that is more calming. Try it; it works. I know, because I am that Mom who was creating those horrific stories in my head, then blowing up as my child walked innocently through the door a few minutes late. The mind is powerful, and if you can change your mind or change your thinking, you really can change your life by reducing your anxiety.

OTHER SUGGESTIONS

If these exercises and techniques don't resonate with you, try taking up a hobby to distract the mind from focusing on things you can't control. Might I suggest you try one of the following?
- Learn to play a musical instrument—guitar, drums, flute, bass, piano, etc.
- Take up a martial art—kung fu, aikido, self-defence, mixed martial arts, etc.
- Join a gym, yoga studio, climbing club, or running club.
- Join a recreational sports team—basketball, football, dodge ball, racquetball, etc.
- Join a book club or visit your local bookstore—it's easy to get lost in a good book.
- Take an art or ceramics class.
- Get exotic with a belly dancing class.
- Play a board game, or solve a puzzle or word game. They're good for the entire family.
- Get outdoors—birdwatching, hiking, canoeing, fishing, four-wheeling, etc.
- Create something with your hands—knitting, cross-stitch, sewing, quilting, woodworking, etc.
- Work with animals—walk the dog, go horseback riding, volunteer at an animal shelter, etc.

CHAPTER 5

To Smoke or Not To Smoke

I don't get it. Billions of dollars have been spent on awareness campaigns regarding the hazards of smoking, yet teens and adults still choose to smoke.

I am not going to ramble on about the hazards of smoking, so this chapter will be short, but it won't be sweet. In my opinion, smoking is a filthy, disgusting habit which only benefits the tobacco industry. However, research has proven that nicotine has the ability to suppress feelings, control one's appetite for food, and help one relax from troubles and feelings of insecurity. Also, smoking is still socially acceptable, although that seems to be changing with the new anti-smoking laws. Whatever the case, smoking is still very attractive to teens, and I want to know why.

Is it simply an act of defiance against authority because laws prohibit anyone under the age of eighteen to purchase cigarettes, or is it because parents say it's not allowed? Do you smoke because all the other kids are doing it? Maybe you tried it once, and now you're hooked. Addictions can happen just that fast for some people.

Why is tobacco so addictive? The reason is that nicotine acts as a stimulant that energizes the body and the mind. The body's tolerance for nicotine rises over time, and more of the substance is required to maintain the same level of energy. Finally, when the body becomes accustomed to the presence of nicotine, it requires the use of the chemical just to help the body function normally. At this point, you have what is commonly known as an addiction.

STOP BEFORE YOU START

So now my dilemma is figuring out how to stop teens before they ever start smoking. For advice on this, I am once again going straight to the source and asking teens. Here is their advice:

- Don't hang out in the smoke pit; eventually you will get sucked into trying a cigarette.
- Some teens say they started smoking pot first, and then advanced to smoking cigarettes. The two just seem to go hand-in-hand for some people, so avoid smoking any substances.
- One girl said that if her friends had thought she looked like a loser, she would never have started smoking. Be a good

friend and tell your buddies who smoke that they look like losers!
- By the way, she also said it had been 7 years since she had quit smoking and she was still fighting the cravings, so do whatever you have to do to avoid that first cigarette.

- Join a sports team. It's great motivation to keep your lungs clean and clear when doing laps in the pool or running suicides.
- Don't emulate your parents. One teen started smoking after curiosity got the best of her after years of watching her parents smoke.
- More confidence would have allowed another teen to stand up for what she believed in, but too much peer pressure and the need to fit in was more powerful than the desire not to smoke. Stand up for what you believe in; you may find you have other friends who believe in the same things you do.

HOW TO SAY *NO*

If I'm going to tell you to just say *no,* then I had better give you a way to save face while doing so. I don't want you to become a social outcast; I just want you to be healthy. Here is some advice from other teens on how to say *no* to smoking:

- Don't say too much when asked if you want a cigarette. There is no explanation and no lecture required. Just say, "No, I'm good." Then keep walking.
- Be direct, don't be vague, or people will keep asking you if you want a smoke. Say something like, "No thanks, it's not for me, but you enjoy."

- This is one instance when it's okay to lie. Tell them "No thanks, I quit", or "Sorry, I'm allergic to smoke".
- Say, "No, I'm not into that." Your friends aren't going to disown you just because you don't want to have a cigarette with them. If the other kids tease you, who cares? If they do, they aren't really your friends anyway.

Do whatever it takes and whatever works to avoid smoking. It's only difficult the first couple of times you have to say *no*; then it gets easier as the other kids get the message. You may even find that others respect you more for your strength in standing up for yourself. Don't be afraid to take a stand against smoking, if that is a choice you've made for your life.

CHAPTER 6

Puff, Puff, Pass

Now, what to say about drugs... Clearly I am against any unnatural substances going into my body; however, teens sometimes have a different view on this subject.

As with all substances, including cigarettes, people use them because they benefit them in some way. They fill a need, though not in a healthy way. What I found from my teen workshops was that the top five substances used by teens, for the most part, were nicotine, marijuana, alcohol, magic mushrooms, and ecstasy. In this chapter we will discuss why teens use these substances, what need is being filled, and what are some healthy alternatives.

The top four reasons for using the various substances were found to be for relaxation, to be less inhibited socially, for relief from physical or emotional pain, and finally, as a way to clear the mind so one can figure out one's life.

Now that we know why teens use drugs, perhaps we can figure out some healthy alternatives. Here are some suggestions:

Relaxation

- Use breathing techniques to allow deep breaths to relax your body and mind. See Chapter 4 on anxiety for this and other relaxation techniques.
- Use meditation which combines deep breathing exercises with relaxation of the mind and body.
- Use energy healing not only for its therapeutic healing properties, but also to provide deep relaxation.
- Take a sauna to deeply relax your muscles.
- Take hot baths, especially with essential oils such as chamomile.
- Take a nice hot shower with lots of steam. It will cleanse and relax you.

Becoming More Social

- Work on the techniques in Chapter 2 for raising self-esteem; with more self-confidence comes increased ease in social settings.

- Concentrate on asking other people questions when in social situations; this takes the focus off you and makes the other person feel that you are interested in what he or she has to say.
- Start to change your belief about not being able to handle yourself in social situations. PSYCH-K is a great energy healing modality for changing beliefs.
- Take workshops that assist teens in becoming more social, for example, workshops on public speaking, etc.
- Work on your own happiness. Do things of a social nature that involve something you are good at or comfortable with, perhaps wall climbing, music camp, dance lessons—whatever makes you happy.

Pain Relief

- Seek out a counsellor. Talking with a psychologist or therapist and getting your emotions out can really help relieve emotional pain.
- Try pet therapy. Your pets are quite happy to sit there and listen to your problems as long as you keep petting them.
- Take your pick from all sorts of natural alternatives for pain relief, ranging from naturopathic medicine, to acupuncture, to energy healing.
- Take up yoga to prevent further injuries or pain.
- Use hot packs and/or cold packs, and topical creams for pain relief.

Figuring Out Your Life

- Meditate so your path becomes clearer to you.

- Take a hot bath in candlelight. This gives you time to slow down and a private place where you can contemplate what is going on in your life.
- Talk to a guidance counsellor and figure out what you may be good at in terms of career choices.
- Talk to a friend and listen to what he or she has experienced. Sometimes a friend can have really good advice.
- Read nonfiction, self-help books and find what resonates with you. Other people have been there, done that, and written a book about it.
- See an intuitive counsellor. This can be a very eye-opening, helpful experience, and just a little bit fun.

Now that you've seen some healthy alternatives to using drugs, I hope that you will consider these healthy options when deciding whether to use drugs or not. Only you can choose what goes into your body. As much as parents would like to think they have control, they really do not. I want you to be prepared to make the best decision for your health and for your life when confronted with this issue. Remember to think about your goals in life when choosing whether or not to use a substance. If using a substance does not get you to your goals, then don't use it. It's far easier to avoid using a substance than to get off it once you start. If you don't believe me, ask any smoker.

WORDS TO LIVE BY

I can't leave this topic without sharing with you a few words of wisdom from the wisest man I've ever known—my grandfather, Gilbert Morand, or as we affectionately called him "Papa". He had three little words that he lived by, and that I now also live by: *Everything In Moderation*. Wise words from a man who lived to be eighty-nine years old and wasn't sick a day in his life. His belief was that extremes were never good; if you stick to moderation, you can experience wonderful things in this life. Here are some of the things he practiced in moderation:

- Drinking is a social activity to be enjoyed in the company of friends and family.
    - We had happy hour at four o'clock every day at my house, when everyone would gather together for a beverage, whether it was alcoholic or not. You were only allowed one drink (although my dad always tried to sneak in a second beer). This was our family time to share a laugh and talk about the day.
- Use as few drugs as possible to get through this life; they only mask the pain and can have damaging side effects.
    - In our house, the strongest drug was coated aspirin. If you had a headache, my mom would send you out for a walk. Recreational drugs were never even heard or spoken of. They were not an option.
- Religion or spirituality should also be practiced in moderation. Excessive religiosity can lead to cults.
    - Believe in something higher than yourself, in whatever form that takes for you, but don't push your beliefs on someone else, and don't take it to extremes.
- Even sports are pretty extreme these days. I can just hear my grandfather saying, "What are these kids thinking?"
    - You are going to need all your joints and other body parts as you get older, so be gentle with your body when playing sports or exercising. Living into your eighties or nineties can seem like a long time when everything hurts.

- Career and business is another area in which to practice moderation.
  - Your family needs to be your top priority. The need to provide was strong for my grandfather, and he sometimes allowed that to rule his life in his younger years. Fortunately, he learned his lesson and was a better grandfather than he was a father.
  - Always lean on your integrity when business is at hand. It's more important that you can sleep at night than to be wildly successful in business.

There was one other point my grandfather was strong on: Laziness is not acceptable, and everyone must pitch in. Share the load, and it won't be so heavy. If everyone pitches in, nobody feels burdened, and life goes on harmoniously.

My grandfather's message is pretty basic but will serve you well if you live by it. The point is to enjoy life, but not at the expense of yourself or others. Party and have a good time, but not to extremes. Have a few drinks if that's what you choose to do, but avoid hard liquor and drugs. Also please, please, please never drink or use drugs and drive. Plan on using a designated driver or leave your car and take a cab if you unexpectedly have a few drinks. Life happens, and sometimes you forget to practice moderation. So, if you party too much, don't make things worse: call a friend or family member to pick you up. There is no shame in being responsible.

CHAPTER 7

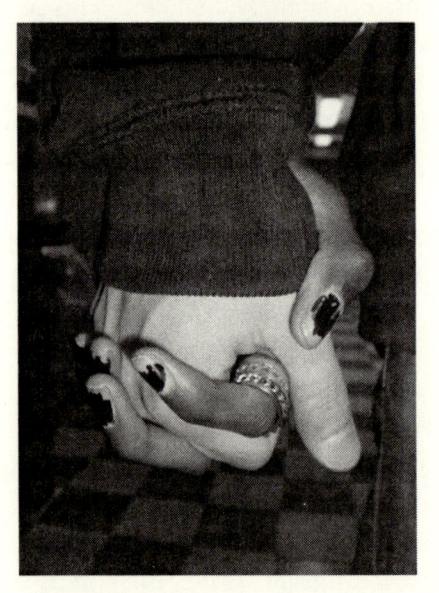

Relationship Remedy

I am going to say this right off the bat, just in case you only read the first paragraph and then move on. If there is only one thing you learn from this chapter, please learn this: Before ever entering into a relationship, first work on yourself. How can you be a good partner for someone else if you don't even love who you are? I truly have a great relationship with myself; I have a super time even when completely on my own. Have you ever heard the saying, "Dance like no one is watching, love like you'll never be hurt, sing like no one is listening, and live like it's heaven on earth"? I definitely try to live by this, but a lot of the time I have to do it in the privacy of my own home. If you're wondering why, you've obviously never heard me sing. Yikes!

I recommend you read this chapter and then reread Chapter 2 on self-esteem to help you work on yourself. Let's now talk about relationships.

TWO MODELS OF A RELATIONSHIP

Which model would you choose?

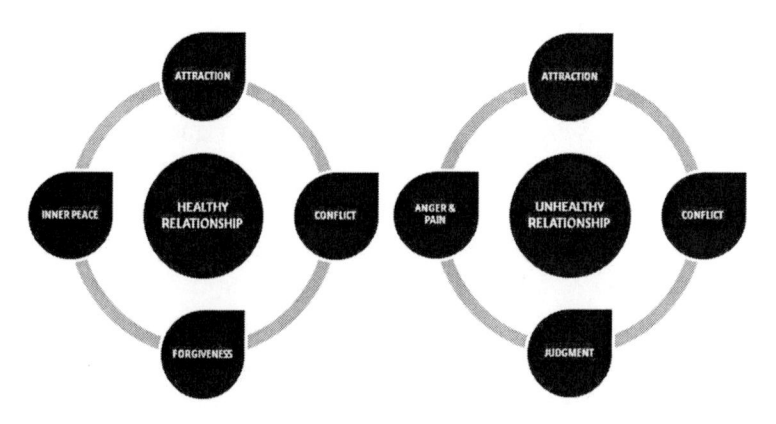

ELEMENTS OF A RELATIONSHIP:
Attraction:
Attraction is that immediate spiritual connection you feel, even before you know anything about the other person. It is a gut feeling one has for someone, not based on looks, social status, or anything physical.

Conflict:
Conflict happens in the course of getting to know the other person, and it happens in any relationship, whether it is healthy or unhealthy. Conflict happens because everyone has different opinions, needs, and experiences.

Forgiveness / Judgment:
Here is where your choice comes into play. You have a choice to live in forgiveness and love, or live in judgment and fear. In the healthy model, you choose to live in love, and in the unhealthy model, you choose to live in fear.

Inner Peace / Anger and Pain:
These are the simple consequences of choosing either forgiveness and love or judgment and fear. Forgiveness leads to inner peace while judgment leads to anger and pain.

Relationships basically come down to deciding whether you want to live your life in forgiveness and love, or judgment and pain. You're probably saying that relationships are more complicated than that, and you are right. However, you do cut through a lot of heartache by following the forgiveness and love model.

There is a universal law called the law of polarity. It states that everything lies on a continuum and has an opposite. We can change undesirable thoughts by concentrating on their opposites. Light, for example, is the opposite of Dark. And Love is the opposite of Fear. Darkness is the absence of Light; Fear is the absence of Love.

This law is most useful in that you can only focus on one polarity at a time. Therefore, we need to choose in each situation whether to live in love or live in fear.

In order for you to better understand this concept, there are a few things you need to understand about fear:
- When people are angry, they are afraid.
- When people are rude, they are afraid.
- When people are manipulative, they are afraid.
- When people are cruel, they are afraid.

If you want to be rid of darkness, you must turn on a light. Similarly, if you want to be rid of fear, you must replace it with love. Let's say your girlfriend just told you she wanted to break up with you. You would probably immediately notice a pain in your stomach or heart and feel your emotions stirring. Now you have a choice to make:

1. Do you want to dwell in anger?
- Continue feeling this pain in your stomach.
- Jump to conclusions about why she is doing this.
- Think that you will never find another person to date as good as she.
- Focus on how mean she is to do this to you.

2. Do you want to forgive her and move on?
- Try to see the situation from her point of view. Why did she feel the need to leave the relationship?
- Understand that not all relationships are meant to last forever, but you are meant to learn something from each relationship. Focus on what the lesson is you were meant to learn.

- Forgive her for not feeling as strongly as you do; it's out of her control.
- Release the pain in your stomach and do something positive for yourself because you are a worthwhile person.

Choosing love doesn't mean you have to become a doormat or aren't allowed to feel upset. It just means you don't choose to dwell in negative or unhappy feelings. Choosing anger and pain can often lead to diseases such as stomach ulcers and migraines when feelings aren't dealt with and released. Anger can blow up into rage when constantly repressed and ignored.

SIGNS OF AN UNHEALTHY RELATIONSHIP
- Too much importance is put on your partner's behaviour, choices, and opinions of you.
- You feel as if you *need* your partner (you have a need that you want him to fill).
- You think the perfect partner will *fix* everything.
- You focus on what you *get* from your partner.
- You think you can fix or change your partner.
- Your partner behaves the way you want him to, never pushes your buttons, or takes you outside your comfort zone (in that case, he is not being honest or communicating his needs).
- You hide your real feelings because of a fear of being judged and not loved.

SIGNS OF A HEALTHY RELATIONSHIP
- You allow your partner to make mistakes and vice versa.
- You *want* to be with that person without *needing* to be with that person.
- You don't care what the other person "brings to the table". You just want him in your life.

- You focus on what you can *give* to your partner.
- You want to support and are quick to forgive your partner.
- Your partner communicates his needs, and supports your growth.
- You feel safe enough to be yourself. You don't feel judged; you know you'll be forgiven.

HOW DO YOU FIND A HEALTHY RELATIONSHIP?

You work on yourself and trust in a higher power or the universe to send that special person along when the time is right. It's all divine timing over which you have no control. And remember, you do not *need* this person to make you happy or whole. If you still feel you do, you have more work to do on yourself. So get ready for Mr. or Ms. Right to come along, by doing the work on yourself.

STOP BLAMING YOUR PARENTS AND EVERYONE ELSE FOR YOUR PROBLEMS!

It's time to take responsibility for your actions and your relationships. Perhaps your mother never told you that you were handsome or beautiful. Stop the pity party now. Understand that hearing this is important in building one's self-esteem, so make sure you compliment others. Your parents did the best job they could, based on their own experiences in life. You are now armed with some really great, life-changing information, but the key is to act on this knowledge. Without action, change will never come.

Practice forgiveness and your relationships will improve. I guarantee it!

CHAPTER 8

Life is Not a Juggling Act

Life is meant to be lived honestly and with integrity. Most people try their best to live this way, but many become trapped in a life of deceit, constantly having to juggle the truth. You may think you don't fall into this category, but I encourage you to read on, as you may someday develop a relationship with this type of person.

THE JUGGLER

Jugglers live their lives juggling three or more balls at a time. These balls represent areas of their lives they keep separate from one another. They may be family, relationships, friends, school, work, etc. Jugglers believe they can keep their family life separate from their school life, and school life separate from friends, and so on.

They also believe it's okay to withhold information or lie about what is going on in other parts of their lives, since these parts are all separate. One part does not affect the others, they believe.

It starts out innocently enough with omissions of the truth, such as skipping classes and trying to hide it from their parents. However, if this type of behaviour isn't changed or kept in check, it can lead to something much more serious as they grow older, such as cheating on their spouse.

This may sound a bit extreme, but life is meant to be played with one ball only. This ball contains all the parts of your life and each part affects the other. The root of the word *integrity* means oneness and wholeness. When you play with only one ball, you have integrity.

If you have three or more balls, all you can do is juggle, but if you only have one ball, you are free to play baseball, basketball, volleyball, dodge ball, jacks—whatever you wish. I think you see what I mean.

Say you want to go out with your friends, but you have a date scheduled with your girlfriend. You can choose to live like the juggler and make up some lame excuse for not going on the date, and then go out with your friends instead, and hope you don't get caught. Or, you can live like a person with integrity, holding one ball. This person would communicate his need to be with his friends and arrange to reschedule his date and make it up to her later. If there is not a constant pattern of blowing off his girlfriend to be with friends, then she should be open and understanding.

LEAVE YOUR JUGGLING DAYS BEHIND

When you live in honesty and integrity and hold only one ball, you will find you are given the trust and freedom to do the things you want in life. However, if you choose to live a life juggling the truth, you will find yourself constantly having to keep an eye on the balls you have in the air. People will not trust you and will try to squash your freedom, because they don't believe or trust what you say.

I want you to be able to play many games with your one ball in the game of life, rather than be limited to a life of juggling. When you juggle, one of those balls is eventually going to fall.

When it does, you will have to make one of three choices
1. Leave the ball on the ground.
2. Replace it with another ball.
3. Pick it back up and try again.

Here is how this would play out in a real life scenario. A man has an affair and falls in love with another woman. His wife finds out about the affair and tells him to make a choice. He has three choices:

Leave the ball on the ground—He asks his wife and family for forgiveness and starts living in honesty and integrity. Eventually, he would leave all the balls on the ground but one.

Replace it with another ball—He chooses this new relationship over the previous one. This can be very problematic, especially when children are involved. The innocent always get hurt in this scenario.

Pick it back up and try again—He keeps trying to juggle and doesn't make the change to honesty and integrity. This decision forces him to continue juggling until the next time he drops the ball, which he eventually will.

Now, you have a choice to make, and that is to be a juggler or a person of integrity. The choice is yours.

CHAPTER 9

Listen to Your Intuition

I am no psychic intuitive, but I have had a lot of luck listening to my intuition. I have learned to trust that little voice inside my head, and *no*, I'm not crazy, everyone has it.

For this section, I am relying on the expertise of my friend, clairvoyant Rosanna Sardella. She is an intuitive consultant and the owner of Emerge Centre for Inner Healing in Calgary, Alberta. She not only does intuitive consulting but also creates and facilitates workshops, including intuitive workshops for teens.

WHAT IS INTUITION?

Here is how *Your Dictionary.com* defines intuition: It is the direct knowing of something without the conscious use of reasoning; immediate understanding; the ability to perceive or know things without conscious reasoning.

This is all true, but what does this mean for you? I believe that everyone is born with a unique gift of knowing. It is a reliable inner resource for wisdom and knowledge that can guide you through life. It's like having an internal "compass" that, if used properly, can lead you to your destination.

Intuition is such a fundamental and intrinsic part of who you are. If you didn't have it, you wouldn't be able to walk, talk, or feel. Your instincts as a baby were very open. Your instinct to "know" when to begin walking and talking was automatic. It's your instincts, your intuition, which help you to evolve, grow, and learn.

If you do not continue to use your "intuition" and instincts, you stop growing, learning, and evolving. I believe this is why many people suffer from depression, anxiety, anger issues, and stress. They have completely shut down their intuition, their internal compass, and are leading lives of disappointment, despair, and hurt.

Of course, children have to conform to the laws and beliefs of their parents, so they have little choice but to "shut down". However, they can change, once they are old enough to make their own decisions. Your intuition is ALWAYS there; it never leaves you, even if you choose to shut it down. When you are ready and willing, the channels open up, and can be developed fully once again—just like when you were a baby.

Using your intuition is a choice. Either you want to or not. It's that simple. You will find that if you choose to use it every day, miracles can and will happen in your life! Not only will you be able to handle and get through challenges and struggles much more easily in life, but you will also be guided to the right people and the right opportunities.

INTUITION=INNER STRENGTH. Once you learn to master your intuition, you can take on the world!

Your intuition manifests itself in different ways:

Dreams

You can receive guidance when you learn to ask for advice in the form of dreams. Before you fall asleep each night, ask your intuition: "Please guide and give me a message about...." Do this nightly, and you will see messages in your dreams. The message could come as a metaphor or a direct answer. Most often it comes as a metaphor. If you are unsure of the meaning, stop analyzing and explore your feelings at that moment. This will help you decipher the dream's meaning. You may also find it helpful to have a "dream meaning" dictionary on hand, to look up the dream's possible meaning.

Inner Voice

It is a still, quiet voice that is always loving and compassionate. It may or may not sound like your own voice. It comes as thoughts in your mind. The positive thoughts are your intuition. The negative thoughts are ego. Most people live in the ego state of mind, meaning the way they were conditioned in life. The ego mind always has a "need", and we feed it by listening to it. The intuition doesn't need anything; that's why it tends to be drowned out by the ego.

Physical Sensations

Intuitive information can come in the form of "a gut feeling", literally a feeling in the pit of your stomach like butterflies (about something good) or nausea and knots (about something bad). Your body may feel heavy if you've made a wrong decision, or it may feel light and experience chills if you've made the right choice. When you feel physically uncomfortable about a situation or person, your intuition is telling you to make a change. When you feel really good and happy, your intuition is telling you that you are on the right path.

Emotions

Intuitive information is often revealed through your feelings or emotions. You may simply "feel right" about a certain person or situation, or you may experience a sense of distrust about an individual or situation. Part of learning to trust your intuition is to ask, "Does this decision make me happy?" or "Do I feel good with this decision?". There are many ways to ask the question and experience the answer, but the truth is simply this: Your intuition will provide you with the information to make positive choices.

Think about why this must be true. Would it make sense for you to have been put here on earth with this magnificent inner guidance system, and every time you trusted it, you felt awful or you made a bad decision? No! If that were the case, you would never use it!

Everyone experiences his or her intuition differently. The next time you need to decide something, ask the question and notice how your intuition conveys the answer to you. You will find your intuition usually speaks to you in the same way.

STEPS TO ACTIVATE YOUR INTUITION

1. Practice by making some low-risk decisions in your life, using your intuition. Ask your intuition: "What do I need to know about this situation or person?" and tune into your feelings. The first thought or feeling is intuitive guidance.
2. Act on the information you receive. Developing your intuition is like learning a new skill. The more you practice, the better you will get at it.
3. Just know that you may not receive the answer right away. If you feel as if you're getting some guidance, but you are still unsure, ask your intuition for more clarification. You may find that the guidance will come later in the day or the next day, when you least expect it!
4. Take small steps in making positive change. Most of us become very anxious and scared when we know we have to make big changes in our lives. It is better to take a small step than no step at all.
5. Write down the guidance you receive. This is a great way to get confirmation on your intuitive guidance. Once you write it down, you can go back and check it after the situation has been resolved and really see how the guidance helped you. Make sure to write down any thoughts, feelings, or body sensations you have at the time.
6. Remember to use your logical, left brain in this process as well. There needn't be competition between the intuitive right side and the logical left side of your brain. Your logical side can help you find out facts and assist you with the details of your decision. Your intuitive side will add that other needed

level of information. Using both for making any decision will make you feel empowered and in control.
7. Most importantly, TRUST the messages you are receiving. You trust by NOT expecting, anticipating, doubting, wondering, or fearing the answers. These feelings only block your ability to truly see, feel, and hear the inner guidance.

YOUR DIVINE COMMUNICATION STYLE—THE FOUR "CLAIRS"

EVERYONE has a capacity to receive divine guidance. It's like tuning into a channel on television. If the channel isn't coming in clearly, you can put up an antenna or adjust the knobs.

Because you are unique, you have your own unique communication style and your own unique way of receiving divine guidance. There are four "channels" of divine communication.

1. Clairvoyance (clear seeing)—seeing pictures that are outside your mind, visions, auras, coloured lights
2. Claircognizance (clear knowing)—suddenly knowing something for a fact, without having any previous knowledge of it, like saying, "I don't know how I know; I just know!"
3. Clairsentience (clear feeling)—receiving guidance through emotions, like having a gut feeling, or through physical sensations like smell, tightened muscles, shivers/goosebumps, or touch
4. Clairaudience (clear hearing)—hearing guidance coming from outside or inside of your mind, a still, small voice from within, gently guiding you (This voice may or may not sound like your own voice.)

Most people have only one or two of these channels open at first. After time and practice, you can open all of your channels. Initially, it's best to focus on fine-tuning the one or two channels you already have open; the other ones will naturally follow.

FINDING YOUR INNER GUIDANCE STYLE

Here's a self-quiz to help you determine your present channels of inner guidance communication. Select the first answer that enters your mind. Don't overthink it; just go with your first thoughts or feelings.
THERE ARE NO RIGHT OR WRONG ANSWERS!

Circle only ONE ANSWER for each question:

1. What you first become aware of about a new friend is
   a. how the person looks, such as hairstyle, facial expressions, or clothing
   b. the sound, tone, of the person's voice
   c. whether or not you feel comfortable about this person
   d. whether or not the person has interesting information to share with you
2. The last movie you really enjoyed had
   a. beautiful scenery
   b. great music
   c. a moving and touching story
   d. an amazing message that made you learn something new
3. Which of these sentences are you most likely to say?
   a. I see what you are saying
   b. I hear what you are saying
   c. this is how I feel about the situation
   d. what do you think about that?

4. Whenever you are solving a dilemma, you are most likely to
   a. imagine different possibilities
   b. talk to yourself, until you come up with a resolution
   c. consider the situation until you get a feeling of peace
   d. wait for an answer to appear in your mind
5. Your ideal career involves
   a. artistic activities such as painting, drawing, photography, architecture, or filming
   b. composing, playing music, or motivational speaking
   c. counselling, writing, dancing
   d. research, science, articles, medicine, inventing
6. What you most love about being in nature is
   a. the beautiful flowers, trees, and surroundings
   b. the sounds of birds, animals, the ocean waves, the wind
   c. the outdoor scents and the fresh air
   d. spending time alone outdoors
7. What others most compliment you on
   a. your physical appearance
   b. your voice
   c. how you feel about yourself
   d. your knowledge
8. If you came across some extra money, the first thing you would do is
   a. buy a painting, a piece of jewellery, a new car
   b. get front-row seats at a concert
   c. go on a rejuvenating retreat with your friends
   d. upgrade your computer system
9. If you could meet any famous or prominent person, you would most want to meet
   a. your favourite actor/actress

b. your favourite musician
c. the author of your favourite book
d. a famous inventor
10. You love to unwind by
a. watching TV or seeing a movie
b. listening to your favourite music
c. getting a massage
d. reading the newspaper or a good book

END OF QUIZ

Now count the number of "a", "b", "c", and "d" answers you've circled.

If you have mostly

- "a" Answers—You are Clairvoyant
- "b" Answers—You are Clairaudient
- "c" Answers—You are Clairsentient
- "d" Answers—You are Claircognizant

PLEASE NOTE: Not one of these orientations is better than the others. They are all just your natural ways of relating to the world around you.

If you have an equal or near-equal number of, say, "b" and "c" answers, this means that you have two wide open channels of divine communication.

Most people have a primary and secondary communication style. Your primary is the one you circled the most, and the secondary is the one you circled second most.

CONGRATULATIONS! Now you can tell the world your style of divine communication!

I want to conclude this chapter by once again urging you to develop and listen to your inner voice of intuition. There will be many situations where the only second opinion you will have is that of your higher self, that voice of intuition. Be ready to filter out the voice of the ego and focus on your intuition for good decision making. You'll know you have made the right decision when there is no internal conflict and everything flows easily. If you make a bad decision, then apologize, make it right if you can, and move on.

The human experience is flawed, and you will make mistakes from time to time. It's what you do with these "mistakes"—I should call them opportunities—that makes all the difference in this world.

CHAPTER 10
Wrapping It Up

People often make life more difficult than it needs to be. The thoughts in your head control your mental and physical well-being. A great attitude goes a long way toward a great life. Let's try a little experiment. I want you to greet everyone you see today with a nice, warm smile and a hello. Your energy will rub off on people and you'll soon see that your smile and your energy become contagious. This is how you can change the world around you. You can make a difference just by adopting a positive attitude. People will want to be around you, and you'll discover what a smile and a positive attitude can attract to your life. So, if anyone asks you why you're so happy today, just tell them it's because you're changing the world, one smile at a time.

I'm sure by now you've gotten the message that you must do the work on yourself. If you are thinking of changing anyone else, you're barking up the wrong tree. You can influence others, but you have no control over them. Positive change has to start with you. You are the only person, place, or thing that is under your control.

As you influence others, so others, of course, influence you—therefore choose your friends and associates wisely—but remember only you can control the decisions you make. Your choices will determine what type of life you lead, whether it will be fulfilling and rewarding, or unfulfilled and boring.

I've used this phrase many times throughout this book, but *the choice is yours*.

Speaking of friends and associates, it's important to realize that we are in fact social creatures and relationships are important to us. You tend to get what you give in social situations, so it's imperative to "love your neighbour as yourself" to quote a phrase from the Good Book. The trick to "loving your neighbour as yourself" is to actually love yourself first. If you don't think you're the most fun, most lovable person you know, then it's time to get to work. How can you love and give to others if you don't love and give to yourself? Aha, they never told you that part, did they? If you don't truly love yourself in the first place, then the phrase *love your neighbour as yourself* is meaningless.

My goal for this book is to open your eyes to your own possibilities and to give you a focus for your future. Knowing what you stand for and where you're headed is important in terms of being successful. Life doesn't always go the way you intend it to, so remember to be flexible and to learn from your experiences. Life is a weird and a wonderful gift; have fun with it. Try not to overanalyze things too much, relax and enjoy. Take a deep breath and seize the day. It is what it is, and will be what you make it. *The choice is yours.* I had to say that just one last time!

REFERENCES

Giedd, Jay N., M.D. (2009, February 26). The Teen Brain: Primed to Learn, Primed to Take Risks. *The Dana Foundation.* Retrieved from http://www.dana.org/news/cerebrum/detail.aspx?id=19620

Winters, Ken C., Ph.D. (2008). Adolescent Brain Development and Drug Abuse. *The Mentor Foundation.* Retrieved from http://www.mentorfoundation.org/uploads/Adolescent_Brain_Booklet.pdf

ABOUT THE AUTHOR
Jane Berthiaume

Jane Berthiaume is a registered clinical hypnotherapist and energy healing practitioner with her own company called Twin Connection Energy Healing Inc., based in Calgary, Alberta. She is the mother of two sons currently in their late teens, Phillip and Nathan, and two adult stepchildren, Natalie and Mike. Jane has created and facilitates a series of workshops designed to teach life skills to teens. Her favourite pastime is spending Friday nights (date night) with her husband, Tim.

ABOUT THE PHOTOGRAPHER/ILLUSTRATOR
Sarah Martensson

Sarah Martensson is a student at Alternative High School in Calgary, Alberta, who attended the series of teen workshops developed by Jane Berthiaume. Sarah is a budding young artist with many talents, including an eye for photography, a love of sketching, a passion for music, and an interest in the healing arts. She jumped at the chance to collaborate with Jane on this book and to give a bit of a teen spin on the photography and artwork. Who better to capture the essence of teenagers than a teen photographer?

Would you like to see your manuscript become a book?

If you are interested in becoming a PublishAmerica author, please submit your manuscript for possible publication to us at:

acquisitions@publishamerica.com

You may also mail in your manuscript to:

**PublishAmerica
PO Box 151
Frederick, MD 21705**

www.publishamerica.com

PUBLISHAMERICA

Breinigsville, PA USA
08 March 2011
257217BV00001B/107/P